Alive in the WORD

CLOUD OF WITNESSES

I0792878

SARAH and HAGAR

Women of Promise

Irene Nowell

Little Rock Scripture Study

A ministry of the Diocese of Little Rock in partnership with Liturgical Press

Nihil obstat: Jerome Kodell, O.S.B., *Censor Librorum.*
Imprimatur: ✠ Anthony B. Taylor, Bishop of Little Rock, April 6, 2016.

Cover design by Ann Blattner. Cover photo: Lightstock. Used with permission.

Photos/illustrations: Page 6, *Abraham and Sarah at the Birth of Isaac*, by Marc Chagall, 1887. Pages 8 (The Code of Hammurabi), 12, 15, 31, and 35, Thinkstock Images by Getty. Page 10, Icon of Abraham and Sarah (detail). Courtesy of Wikimedia Commons. Page 16, Abraham detail from a window at Saint Vitus Cathedral, Prague. Photo by Gene Plaisted, OSC, © The Crosiers. Used with permission. Page 20, Tomb of Sarah in Hebron. Courtesy of Wikimedia Commons. Page 27, *Abraham's Counsel to Sarah*, by James Tissot. Jewish Museum, New York. Courtesy of Wikimedia Commons. Page 34, Icon of Abraham's Visitors (*Trinity*), by Andrei Rublyov, 1425. Courtesy of Wikimedia Commons.

Scripture texts, prefaces, introductions, footnotes, and cross-references used in this work are taken from the *New American Bible, revised edition* © 2010, 1991, 1986, 1970 Confraternity of Christian Doctrine, Washington, DC and are used by permission of the copyright owner. All Rights Reserved. No part of the New American Bible may be reproduced in any form without permission in writing from the copyright owner.

© 2016 by Little Rock Scripture Study, Little Rock, Arkansas. All rights reserved. No part of this book may be reproduced in any form or by any means without the written permission of the copyright holder. Published by Liturgical Press, Collegeville, Minnesota 56321. Printed in the United States of America.

ISBN: 978-0-8146-3618-3 (print); 978-0-8146-4627-4 (ebook)

Contents

Introduction

Alive in the Word brings you resources to deepen your understanding of Scripture, offer meaning for your life today, and help you to pray and act in response to God's word.

Use any volume of **Alive in the Word** in the way best suited to you.

- **For individual learning and reflection**, consider this an invitation to prayerfully journal in response to the questions you find along the way. And be prepared to move from head to heart and then to action.
- **For group learning and reflection**, arrange for three sessions where you will use the material provided as the basis for faith sharing and prayer. You may ask group members to read each chapter in advance and come prepared with questions answered. In this kind of session, plan to be together for about an hour. Or, if your group prefers, read and respond to the questions together without advance preparation. With this approach, it's helpful to plan on spending more time for each group session in order to adequately work through each chapter.

- **For a parish-wide event or use within a larger group,** provide each person with a copy of this volume, and allow time during the event for quiet reading, group discussion and prayer, and then a final commitment by each person to some simple action in response to what he or she learned.

This volume explores the theme of **A Cloud of Witnesses.** The pages of our Bibles are filled with the stories of women and men who have played a unique role in salvation history. By entering into a few key biblical passages written by or describing these people, we begin to see how our own story continues God's great work of salvation in the world. Their witness, handed on to us from centuries ago, continues to speak to us and challenge us to stand as faithful witnesses in today's world.

Sarah and Hagar

Begin by asking God to assist you in your prayer and study. Then read through Genesis 16:1-10, our introduction to Sarah and her husband Abraham.

Genesis 16:1-10
1 Abram's wife Sarai had borne
him no children. Now she had
an Egyptian maidservant named
Hagar. 2 Sarai said to Abram:
"The LORD has kept me from
bearing children. Have inter-
course with my maid; perhaps I
will have sons through her." Abram obeyed Sarai. 3 Thus, after
Abram had lived ten years in the land of Canaan, his wife
Sarai took her maid, Hagar the Egyptian, and gave her to her
husband Abram to be his wife. 4 He had intercourse with her,
and she became pregnant. As soon as Hagar knew she was
pregnant, her mistress lost stature in her eyes. 5 So Sarai said
to Abram: "This outrage against me is your fault. I myself
gave my maid to your embrace; but ever since she knew she
was pregnant, I have lost stature in her eyes. May the LORD
decide between you and me!" 6 Abram told Sarai: "Your maid
is in your power. Do to her what you regard as right." Sarai
then mistreated her so much that Hagar ran away from her.

7The LORD's angel found her by a spring in the
wilderness, the spring on the road to Shur, 8and
he asked, "Hagar, maid of Sarai, where have you
come from and where are you going?" She an-
swered, "I am running away from my mistress,
Sarai." 9But the LORD's angel told her: "Go back
to your mistress and submit to her authority.
10I will make your descendants so numerous,"
added the LORD's angel, "that they will be too
many to count."

Setting the Scene

Two women are the main characters in this scene. The first is Sarai (Sarah), wife of Abram (Abraham). She appears first as part of a genealogy introducing Abraham and his family. The father of every person in this genealogy is named except for Sarah. The only information given is that she is the wife of Abraham and that she has no child (Gen 11:27-30). As the story progresses she will travel with Abraham wherever God calls him. She will also be pawned off to Pharaoh as his sister, but God protects her (Gen 12:11-20). Technically Abraham is correct even though he intends to deceive Pharaoh. "Sister" (Hebrew *'achoth*) is a common term for "wife" in the Old Testament (see Song 4:9-10; 5:1; Tob 5:21; 7:15). Also in a later incident where he makes the same claim he says Sarah is his "father's daughter, not [his] mother's" (Gen 20:12). This kind of relationship will later be forbidden (see Deut 27:22).

The reader is reminded frequently that Sarah has no child. Her barrenness is a major problem, because God has promised Abraham twice that he will be the ancestor of a great nation, living in their own land, with descendants as many as the stars (Gen 12:2; 15:5). It was also commonly believed in the ancient world that the lack of children was due to the wife's barrenness, not the husband's infertility.

The other woman is Hagar, Sarah's maidservant. Hagar is an Egyptian, which leads to the question: was Hagar one of the female servants that Pharaoh gave Abraham after the incident when he claimed Sarah was his sister (Gen 12:16)? Sarah will use Hagar to solve her problem of barrenness. In the ancient world it was not uncommon for maids to be used as surrogate mothers. A man needed sons so his line would be preserved. There was no clear belief in life after death at the time of Abraham, so the only way a person lived on was through children, especially sons. If God is going to be faithful to Abraham regarding the covenant promises, there must be sons. It seems impossible that he will beget sons through Sarah, so the maid will be called upon to provide.

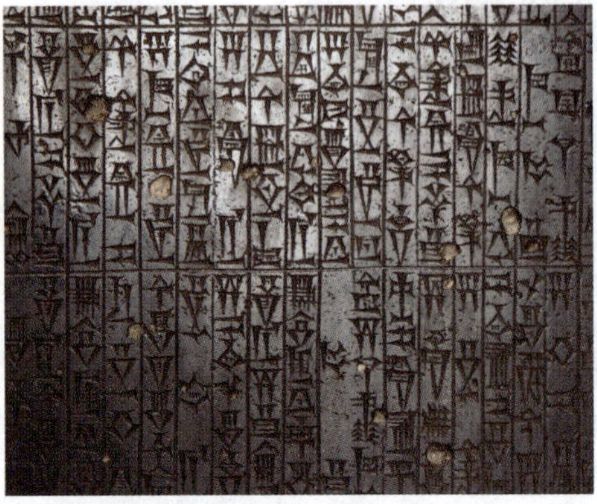

Code of Hammurabi

The relationship between Sarah, Hagar, and Abraham now becomes ambiguous. In the ancient law codes the child conceived by the maid is regarded as the son of the wife. According to the code of Hammurabi (eighteenth century BC), the maid or slave cannot consider herself a second wife and does not have the same legal rights as the wife. So according to this law and custom Sarah should be considered the mother of Hagar's son. Another complication arises, however, from the title given to Hagar. In Genesis 16:3 she is called Abraham's "wife" (Hebrew *'ishshah*), not a maid or concubine (Hebrew *pilegesh*). For a man to have more than one wife was also accepted in the ancient world. So is Hagar now a surrogate mother and is her son really Sarah's? Or is she a second wife with her own rights? The biblical text does not clarify.

The entire passage will be considered a few verses at a time. The occasional questions in the margin are for discussion with others. If you are using these materials on your own, use the questions for personal reflection or as a guide to journaling.

Understanding the Scene Itself

1 Abram's wife Sarai had borne him no children.
Now she had an Egyptian maidservant named
Hagar. 2 Sarai said to Abram: "The Lord has
kept me from bearing children. Have intercourse with my maid; perhaps I will have sons through her." Abram obeyed Sarai.

The initial conversation between Abraham and Sarah seems both friendly and practical. We have no sons, so do what ancient Mesopotamian law recommends: use your maid as a surrogate

mother. It is noteworthy that the suggestion is made, not by Abraham, but by Sarah. Sarah also observes that it is the Lord who has prevented her from getting pregnant and bearing children. The whole mystery of how life begins and new human beings are conceived and born is in the hands of God. Human beings can take some action, but ultimately it is God who creates the new person. Sarah is well aware of this truth and so also lays the blame for her barrenness on God.

It is also noteworthy that Abraham obeys Sarah. There is a mutuality in the relationship between husband and wife. Sarah takes the initiative to propose a solution to their difficulty, and Abraham obeys her. Throughout this passage Sarah is the one in charge. Sarah also assumes at this point that the custom of using a maid as a surrogate mother will work to her advantage. She expects that the sons born to Hagar will be considered children of Sarah.

In what way are you able to relate to Sarah's predicament? Is there a situation in your life where you might both wait and take action?

3Thus, after Abram had lived ten years in the land of Canaan, his wife Sarai took her maid, Hagar the Egyptian, and gave her to her husband Abram to be his wife.
4He had intercourse with her, and she became pregnant. As soon as Hagar knew she was pregnant, her mistress lost stature in her eyes.

Trouble appears already in verse 3. Sarah takes action, as she and Abraham had agreed. But a subtle change in wording changes everything. Sarah gives Hagar to Abraham, but not as a surrogate mother. She gives Hagar to Abraham "to be his wife." Hagar's status has already been transformed. She is no longer a maid; she is a second wife. Now, according to ancient Near Eastern law and custom, she has rights that she did not have before. This situation is not going to work out well for Sarah.

Abraham impregnates Hagar promptly. This piece of news confirms the supposition that it is Sarah who is infertile, not Abraham. In just four Hebrew words Hagar has become the mother of Abraham's child. Hagar realizes well that her status has changed. She sees herself as a second wife; she is the mother of the master's son. Sarah, on the other hand, has lost status. Sarah is the older, barren, first wife who has no children. Hagar apparently loses no time in reminding her "former" mistress of this new situation.

5So Sarai said to Abram: "This outrage against me is your fault. I myself gave my maid to your embrace; but ever since she knew she was pregnant, I have lost stature in her eyes. May the LORD decide between you and me!" 6Abram told Sarai: "Your maid is in your power. Do to her what you regard as right." Sarai then mistreated her so much that Hagar ran away from her.

The proverbial saying, "Be careful what you wish for or desire" could be applied to Sarah's situation. When have your own plans had unintended or opposite effects? Any lessons learned?

Sarah blames Abraham for this distressing situation. In one sense she is right. Abraham has impregnated Hagar and fathered her child. But Sarah is the person who suggested this solution to their problem and who gave Hagar to Abraham "as a wife." In her frustration Sarah has shifted all the responsibility to Abraham and now she calls on God to resolve the difficulty. Abraham, for his part, still insists that the responsibility and the power belong to Sarah. She can do whatever she wishes to her maid. Notice that Hagar is Sarah's maid even as she is Abraham's second wife. Sarah and Abraham both continue throughout the passage to call Hagar a maid (Gen 16:1 [2x], 2, 3, 5, 6, 8; Hebrew *shiphhah)*. Sarah then proceeds to drive Hagar away.

**7The LORD's angel found her by a spring in the
wilderness, the spring on the road to Shur, 8and
he asked, "Hagar, maid of Sarai, where have you
come from and where are you going?" She answered, "I am running away from my mistress,**

Sarai." 9But the LORD's angel told her: "Go back
to your mistress and submit to her authority. 10I
will make your descendants so numerous,"
added the LORD's angel, "that they will be too
many to count."

For the first time in this passage, God takes an active part. Sarah accused the Lord of not giving her children but God made no response. Now that Hagar has run away from Sarah and Abraham, God comes in the form of an angel to comfort Hagar and to give her a significant message. God addresses Hagar by name and by status, maid of Sarah. Then God asks a very important question: "Where have you come from and where are you going?" Hagar shows no fear but responds honestly: "I am running away." God, however, has other plans for Hagar and sends her back to the difficult situation. But God does not send her empty. God gives her the same promise that God has given Abraham: descendants so numerous that they will be impossible to count (see Gen 15:5).

If there is a situation in your life that makes you feel justified in fleeing, are you prepared to stop, reflect, and listen before acting? What disciplines might help you face the situation with courage?

God's words to Hagar may be seen as an instruction to us too. Many times we need to stop and hear God's question: "Where have you come from and where are you going?" Running away may seem to be a solution to conflict, but it rarely is. God may indeed be sending us back to face the situation. Having the courage to stop and listen to God is an initial step toward growth in our relationships to one another and to God. Hagar is our model here. As the passage continues, Hagar gives God a name: "You are God who sees me" (Gen 16:13). She is the first person in Scripture to name God. The promise God has given her follows a repeated form of announcing the birth of an important son. The same form is used in the announcement to Mary of the birth of Jesus (Luke 1:29-38; see Luke 1:11-20). Hagar clearly is important to God.

What about Sarah? She will be compelled to recognize Hagar's worth and to accept Hagar's son into the family. As Deuteronomy says:

> If a man has two wives, one loved and the other unloved, and if both the loved and the unloved bear him sons, but the first-born is the son of the unloved wife: when he comes to bequeath his property to his sons he may not consider as his firstborn the son of the wife he loves, in preference to the son of the wife he does not love, the firstborn. On the contrary, he shall recognize as his firstborn the son of the unloved wife, giving him a double share of whatever he happens to own, since he is the first fruits of his manhood, and to him belong the rights of the firstborn (Deut 21:15-17).

But Hagar's return to Sarah will not result in reconciliation. The tension between the two women will only be heightened by further developments.

Praying the Word / Sacred Reading

Return to the full passage (Gen 16:1-10) and read it aloud. As you do so, what words or phrases

stand out to you? Jot down and use these words or phrases as a way to prayerfully consider that God might be catching your attention in a particular way or for a particular purpose at this time. Allow the words that "spoke to you" to become a springboard to you to speak to God. And be prepared to spend some time in silence listening for even a small still voice as God speaks to your heart.

Living the Word

Consider one of the following:

- Spend time with someone this week whose life circumstances make him or her vulnerable to the wishes and desires of others. Is there a Hagar in your midst?
- What descriptive name might you use for God that reflects your experience of God's work in your life? Use this name for God in prayer this week.

The Blessing of Sarah's Fertility

Begin again by asking God to assist you in your prayer and study. Then read through Genesis 17:15-21, an account of God's promise to bless Abraham and Sarah with a child with a future full of promise.

Genesis 17:15-21
15God further said to Abraham:
As for Sarai your wife, do not
call her Sarai; her name will be
Sarah. 16I will bless her, and I will
give you a son by her. Her also
will I bless; she will give rise to nations, and rulers of peoples
will issue from her. 17Abraham fell face down and laughed as
he said to himself, "Can a child be born to a man who is a
hundred years old? Can Sarah give birth at ninety?" 18So
Abraham said to God, "If only Ishmael could live in your
favor!" 19God replied: Even so, your wife Sarah is to bear you
a son, and you shall call him Isaac. It is with him that I will
maintain my covenant as an everlasting covenant and with
his descendants after him. 20Now as for Ishmael, I will heed
you: I hereby bless him. I will make him fertile and will mul-
tiply him exceedingly. He will become the father of twelve
chieftains, and I will make of him a great nation. 21But my

covenant I will maintain with Isaac, whom Sarah shall bear to you by this time next year.

Setting the Scene

The story of Abraham and Sarah was told in several versions and the ancient editors apparently did not want to lose any of them. Thus we have again God's promise to make a covenant agreement with Abraham and to bless him with many descendants (see also Gen 12:1-3; 15:1-19; 17:1-14). In response to all these divine promises, Abraham believes, even though on occasion he asks pertinent questions as he does in this passage. This version of the story is attributed to a group of storytellers called "Priestly" because their interests have to do with sacrificial worship, genealogies, and God's ongoing faithfulness to the promises.

God honors the covenant by promising to bless Abraham and his family (Gen 17:16; see 12:2; 18:18). "Bless" (Hebrew *barak*) is a powerful concept in the Old Testament. It implies a sharing in God's life and power. In the Genesis 1 creation story God blesses the human beings with the power to continue creation and to care for it as God intends: "Be fertile and multiply; fill the earth and subdue it" (Gen 1:28; see Gen 9:1). In the first conversation with Abraham God uses the words "bless" and "blessing" five times, twice in Genesis 12:2 and three times in Genesis 12:3. God's blessing will enable Abraham to become a great nation and to bring blessing to all the families of the earth (Gen 12:2-3). God's promise of blessing continues in Genesis 17 and in this chapter Sarah is also blessed (Gen 17:16).

The story in Genesis 17:15-21 is told following a birth announcement form that is repeated frequently in these ancestor stories. The elements that appear in this form are these:

- an appearance of the Lord or of an angel representing the Lord (see Gen 17:1-2, 15);
- the human response of fear and/or reverence (see Gen 17:3);
- a promise from God that a son will be born (see Gen 17:16);
- the human response that this is impossible (see Gen 17:17); and
- God's reassurance (see Gen 17:19).

Often the name of the son is given and his future is described.

Christians are familiar with this form because of Gabriel's announcement to Mary that she will have a son and will call his name Jesus (Luke 1:26-38). A similar announcement was given to Zechariah concerning the birth of John the Baptist (Luke 1:5-20). An abbreviated announcement of birth was given to Hagar in Genesis 16:7-12.

The names of people are significant also in this ancestral story. In Genesis 17 both Abram and Sarai receive new names. Even though their new names are only variants of their old ones, these new names are interpreted to have an added meaning. God changes Abram's name to Abraham, meaning "the father [*'ab*] is exalted" (Gen 17:5). Sarai's name is changed to Sarah, meaning "princess" (Gen 17:15). The third name that appears is the name of their child, Isaac, in Hebrew *yishaq*. This name has an even greater significance; it means "laughter." In this birth announcement story Abraham laughs (Gen 17:17). In the following story Sarah will laugh (Gen 18:12-15). When their promised child is born, it is not surprising that they name their child "Laughter." They are delighted in this marvelous turn of events.

Considering the significance of assigning names in the Bible, do you know if your name has a spiritual meaning?

Before Isaac arrives, however, Abraham is not sure that a new baby is a good idea. Abraham loves Hagar's son Ishmael. He has waited long enough for a son and now he is satisfied with the child he already has (Gen 17:18). But God has greater plans for this younger promised son who will be named Isaac. Nonetheless God reassures Abraham that Ishmael will also be blessed and will also become the father of twelve sons and the ancestor of a great nation (Gen 17:20). Abraham's love for Ishmael will continue to cause problems in the family. Sarah will eventually force Abraham to drive Ishmael and Hagar away (Gen 21:9-19). But the relationship is not totally broken. After God tests Abraham by asking him to offer Isaac as a sacrifice and then reversing the request when Abraham is prepared to obey (Gen 22:1-18), Abraham does not return to Hebron where Sarah apparently is, but travels to Beer-sheba where Hagar and Ishmael live (Gen 22:19; see Gen 21:14). Abraham returns to Hebron only to bury Sarah (Gen 23:2). The struggle for descendants seems to have divided the family.

Tomb of Sarah in Hebron

The entire passage will be considered a few verses at a time. The occasional questions may be used in group discussion or for your own personal reflection.

Understanding the Scene Itself

15God further said to Abraham: As for Sarai your wife, do not call her Sarai; her name will be Sarah. 16I will bless her, and I will give you a son by her. Her also will I bless; she will give rise to nations, and rulers of peoples will issue from her.

The gift of a name is always significant. Parents sometimes name their children after other relatives or for famous people, hoping the child will grow to be as good or successful or noteworthy as the other person. Saints' names are given at baptism with a prayer that the patron will protect the child and lead him or her to holiness. At marriage wives often take the name of their husbands or, less often, husbands the name of their wives. The new name signifies a new status. The same practice is often seen in religious communities, also signifying a new identity.

God has already changed Abram's name to Abraham (Gen 17:5) and now gives Sarai a new name also, Sarah. The identity of both is being transformed as they are prepared to be the ancestors of God's chosen people. God not only blesses Abraham but also blesses Sarah, giving her too a share in God's life and power. God will work through her as well as through Abraham to form a special people.

Blessing implies a share in God's life and power.

[17]Abraham fell face down and laughed as he said to himself, "Can a child be born to a man who is a hundred years old? Can Sarah give birth at ninety?" [18]So Abraham said to God, "If only Ishmael could live in your favor!"

Abraham still thinks that the mother of the chosen people will be Hagar. He has formed a bond with his only child, Ishmael. The struggle between Sarah and Hagar has taken its toll on Abraham also. So he pleads with God to choose Hagar's son as the father of the promised descendants. He is tired and cannot face more impossibilities. But God has not only chosen Abraham; God has also chosen Sarah, even if she is ninety years old. God is not daunted by the age of the parents. God is completely free to bring new life into the world, however impossible it seems in human eyes. God is often slow in fulfilling

Where have you seen evidence of God's ability to bring new life into the world?

promises, but God remains faithful. Here God is faithful not only to Abraham, who has heard the promise several times, but also to Sarah, who has just received the promise of giving "rise to nations." The task for the human participants in this drama is to cling to the promise in faith, no matter how long they have to wait.

What "impossible" situation are you surrendering to God's care?

19God replied: Even so, your wife Sarah is to bear you a son, and you shall call him Isaac. It is with him that I will maintain my covenant as an everlasting covenant and with his descendants after him.

God now states directly that this covenant will be maintained with Sarah's son, not Hagar's. Even though God spoke directly to Hagar and has never spoken to Sarah, it is Sarah who is mother of the promise. Her son, who is to be named Isaac, will maintain the covenant with God and bequeath it to the coming generations into eternity. Isaac's name is significant; it means "laughter." Abraham laughed when he heard that he would have another son and that this son would be borne by Sarah. Laughter will appear again in the next chapter. This promised son will never let his parents forget their laughter, whether it was in disbelief or delight. Isaac, "Laughter," is the fulfillment of God's promise.

[20]Now as for Ishmael, I will heed you: I hereby bless him. I will make him fertile and will multiply him exceedingly. He will become the father of twelve chieftains, and I will make of him a great nation.

God has not forgotten Ishmael, however. He too is a son of Abraham. God also blesses him with a share in divine life and power. In the beginning God said, "be fertile and multiply" (see Gen 1:28). God repeated this blessing to Noah (Gen 9:1, 7). Now God promises the same blessing to Ishmael. He too will be the father of twelve sons, just as Abraham's grandson, Jacob, will be. He too will be a great nation. He too will be marked with the sign of the covenant, circumcision (Gen 17:25). As the story progresses, however, the relationship between the descendants of Isaac and Ishmael will not always be happy.

[21]But my covenant I will maintain with Isaac, whom Sarah shall bear to you by this time next year.

For the first time in this story of anticipated pregnancies God reveals a time frame. About a year from this time Sarah will give birth to a son. It has been a long time since the journey of Abraham and Sarah from Mesopotamia to Canaan, from there to Egypt and back again. The promise to Abraham has been renewed over and over: "You will be the ancestor of a mighty nation." But year after year nothing has happened.

Abraham pointed this out to God and complained that all the promises would be worthless if he died childless (Gen 15:2). But God reassured him and he believed. This faith was credited to Abraham as righteousness (Gen 15:6). Still nothing happened, so Sarah and Abraham decide to use a surrogate mother to force God's hand, it seems (Gen 16). Hagar does indeed give birth to Abraham's son, and Abraham thinks the promise has been fulfilled. But God has other plans. The promised son, who will be the ancestor of nations and the bearer of an eternal covenant, will be a child of Sarah. Within a year Sarah will give birth to this son who will be the heir of God's covenant with Abraham. Abraham, however, is still keeping his options open. He has Ishmael, Hagar's son, circumcised (Gen 17:23-26). Thus Ishmael bears the sign of the covenant just as Abraham does.

In your life, is there an "Ishmael" figure, someone who enjoys God's favor even if not the one to receive top billing?

Throughout this chapter, however, God has insisted that Ishmael is not the heir. The heir to God's promises and the bearer of God's covenant into the future will be, not a son of Hagar, but a son of Sarah. Even though God never speaks to Sarah, God honors her too with a promise of covenant and of heirs to continue that covenant. She is indeed the mother of the promise.

Praying the Word / Sacred Reading

These words may be used for your own prayer or you may choose to use your own words or even silence in response to the story from Genesis 17:15-21.

God of life, we lift our hearts to you, as we pray for all people:

> For those who patiently face disappointment
> and for those who do not.
> For those who plead with you for answers
> and for those who have given up.
> For those who are oppressed and exploited
> and for their oppressors.
> For those whose blessings are obvious
> and for those whose blessings we do not see.
> For those who act in faith and humility
> and for those whose pride is an obstacle to faith.

Gather us, O God, so that together we may give expression to your creative love. Tear down what divides us; heal what frightens us; correct what oppresses us. Draw us to yourself to receive your blessing and to become an avenue for your power in our world.

Living the Word

The stories of Sarah and Hagar and Abraham often emphasize the blessing that God generously shares regardless of one's virtue or worthiness or accomplishments. It is humbling to know that God's generosity comes without our deserving it. How might such awareness make you better able to bear God's blessing to others? Who do you work with or live with who might be in need of experiencing God's blessing? How will your presence, your words, your actions communicate this blessing to them?

The Lord Visits the Dwelling in Mamre

Invite God to assist you in your prayer and study. Then read the following passage from Genesis 18:1-15.

Genesis 18:1-15
1The LORD appeared to
Abraham by the oak of
Mamre, as he sat in the
entrance of his tent, while
the day was growing hot.
2Looking up, he saw three
men standing near him.
When he saw them, he
ran from the entrance of the tent to greet them; and bowing to
the ground, 3he said: "Sir, if it please you, do not go on past
your servant. 4Let some water be brought, that you may bathe
your feet, and then rest under the tree. 5Now that you have
come to your servant, let me bring you a little food, that you
may refresh yourselves; and afterward you may go on your
way." "Very well," they replied, "do as you have said."

6Abraham hurried into the tent to Sarah and said, "Quick,
three measures of bran flour! Knead it and make bread." 7He

ran to the herd, picked out a tender, choice calf,
and gave it to a servant, who quickly prepared
it. [8]Then he got some curds and milk, as well as
the calf that had been prepared, and set these
before them, waiting on them under the tree
while they ate.
[9]"Where is your wife Sarah?" they asked him.
"There in the tent," he replied. [10]One of them said,
"I will return to you about this time next year, and
Sarah will then have a son." Sarah was listening
at the entrance of the tent, just behind him. [11]Now
Abraham and Sarah were old, advanced in years,
and Sarah had stopped having her menstrual pe-
riods. [12]So Sarah laughed to herself and said,
"Now that I am worn out and my husband is old,
am I still to have sexual pleasure?" [13]But the LORD
said to Abraham: "Why did Sarah laugh and say,
'Will I really bear a child, old as I am?' [14]Is any-
thing too marvelous for the LORD to do? At the
appointed time, about this time next year, I will
return to you, and Sarah will have a son." [15]Sarah
lied, saying, "I did not laugh," because she was
afraid. But he said, "Yes, you did."

Setting the Scene

The reader has certainly noticed that some of these stories seem to repeat. For example, the announcement of birth appears yet again in Genesis 18. The first appearance of this form was to Hagar, when the angel announced the impending birth of Ishmael (Gen 16:7-12). The second announcement was to Abraham, announcing the birth of Isaac (Gen 17:15-19). Now God repeats the announcement to Abraham (Gen 18:1-15). The two announcements of Isaac's birth are different in style even as they repeat the same message in basically the same form. The event in Genesis 17 is more formal. God appears to him and declares his name, "God the Almighty," *El Shaddai* in Hebrew. This name is perhaps the most ancient term for God (Gen 17:1). God establishes the covenant, calls for the covenant sign of circumcision, and announces the future birth of Sarah's child. The story in Genesis 18 is more informal and homey. The reader is told immediately that this is "the LORD" who is appearing to Abraham. God is identified by the proper name, "the LORD," YHWH in Hebrew. (The small capital letters in the word "LORD" indicate the underlying Hebrew.) Abraham, however, sees only three men and offers them hospitality. This repetition of information in different styles reveals again the weaving together of different versions of the story. The ancient editors respected the different versions and, not wanting to lose anything, kept portions of each. The more informal version is known as the Yahwist version because of its use of God's proper name. The more formal version is probably the more recent and is known as the Priestly version because it is thought that it was written by the priests.

A second pattern that repeats is what is called the "wife-sister" stories. The first appearance of this form is in Genesis 12, and was described in the discussion of Genesis 16. It will appear again in Genesis 20 at a much more critical moment. In Genesis 17 and 18 Abraham has been told

By using repetition and story patterns, the biblical storytellers show themselves to be masters of their craft. When has a sacred story touch your heart? How do such stories reveal God's persistence to you?

that it is Sarah who will be the mother of the promised son and that she will give birth within the year (Gen 17:15-19, 21; 18:10, 14). The birth of this promised son is told in Genesis 21. In Genesis 20, however, Abraham is again an alien in a strange place, Gerar. Again he identifies Sarah as his sister and King Abimelech takes her into his harem. But God warns Abimelech in a dream that Sarah is Abraham's wife. God has protected Sarah and Abimelech by not allowing the king to touch her. Abimelech scolds Abraham, who defends himself by saying that Sarah is indeed his father's daughter but not his mother's. Abimelech gives presents to Abraham as a testimony to Sarah's honor. This repeated threat to Sarah is significant because Isaac will be born in the next chapter, Genesis 21. The reader must be reassured that Isaac is truly Abraham's son and not Abimelech's. The promise of descendants is not fulfilled easily. Its success is threatened several times. But finally the promised son of Abraham is born to Sarah. God has overcome the threats and fulfilled the promise.

In Genesis 18 Abraham and Sarah are living at Mamre, a place only named in connection to Abraham. It seems to be close to or the same as Hebron, but the two names are never used together. Abraham settles there after he and his nephew Lot separate (Gen 13:18). Abraham is "camping at the oak of Mamre the Amorite" when the chiefs of the land take Lot captive (Gen 14:13). After Abraham defeats the kings and rescues Lot, he refuses to take any of the plunder except what is due to his allies, including the

Amorite named Mamre (Gen 14:24). The place, Mamre, is thus named for the Amorite who is an ally of Abraham. A third name for this place is Kiriath-arba. Sarah "died in Kiriath-arba—now Hebron—in the land of Canaan" (Gen 23:1). It is here that Abraham buys the field and the cave to use as a burial place for his family (Gen 23:17-20). This is the only land Abraham ever owns. Here Abraham is buried "in the field . . . which faces Mamre" (Gen 25:9). To this place Jacob returns with his family after his sojourn with Laban (Gen 35:27). Here Jacob too is buried (Gen 49:30; 50:13).

The entire passage will be considered a few verses at a time. Use the occasional questions for group discussion or for your own personal reflection.

Understanding the Scene Itself

**[1]The LORD appeared to Abraham by the oak of
Mamre, as he sat in the entrance of his tent,
while the day was growing hot. [2]Looking up, he
saw three men standing near him. When he saw**

them, he ran from the entrance of the tent to greet them; and bowing to the ground. . . .

The scene portrays what seems to be an ordinary day in a desert summer. The heat is oppressive so Abraham is sitting at the entrance of his tent, perhaps hoping to catch a breeze. Then he glimpses three men standing near him. The verb catches our attention. The men are not walking toward him, but they are standing nearby. How did Abraham miss their approach? Their sudden appearance is the first clue that these are not ordinary men and this is not an ordinary arrival. Abraham is immediately attentive. He runs to meet the men, greets them, and bows to the ground before them in reverence. His action shows the depth of his respect for every human being. This respect and care for others is characteristic of desert people to this day. No one can survive in the desert alone, and so the people who live there are eager to assist any travelers who appear.

The reader, however, has an immediate clue regarding the identity of these three strangers. It is "the LORD" who has mysteriously appeared to Abraham in the person of these three men. As the story unfolds, one of the men will be identified as "the LORD" (Gen 18:13) and in a later incident the other two "men" will be identified as angels (Gen 19:1).

[3]He said: "Sir, if it please you, do not go on past your servant. [4]Let some water be brought, that you may bathe your feet, and then rest under the

tree. [5]Now that you have come to your servant, let me bring you a little food, that you may refresh yourselves; and afterward you may go on your way." "Very well," they replied, "do as you have said."

The author of Hebrews later recalled this Genesis scene, saying, "Do not neglect hospitality, for through it some have unknowingly entertained angels" (Heb 13:2). When have you experienced hospitality as a time of grace?

Abraham offers the three strangers all the gifts of hospitality that he has available. He invites them to stay and rest in the shade of his tree. He provides water for them to wash the dust and sand from their feet. He promises to provide "a little food." Then, rested and strengthened for their journey, he will send them on their way. He repeatedly calls himself their "servant." He will wait on them as long as they are at his tent. The men agree to his offer. It must be noted, however, that Abraham is not providing all this hospitality on his own. The water to wash the men's feet will "be brought," apparently by a servant. The "little food" will also not be prepared by Abraham himself.

[6]Abraham hurried into the tent to Sarah and said, "Quick, three measures of bran flour! Knead it and make bread." [7]He ran to the herd, picked out a tender, choice calf, and gave it to a servant, who quickly prepared it. [8]Then he got some curds and milk, as well as the calf that had been prepared, and set these before them, waiting on them under the tree while they ate.

The next paragraph introduces those who will do the work of providing the hospitality. Abraham is clearly in a hurry. First he goes into the

tent to enlist Sarah to help him. He gives the orders in two brief commands consisting of only eight words in Hebrew. Then he runs to his herd of animals, chooses the best calf himself, and gives it to a servant. The servant prepares the calf "quickly." Abraham's haste shows his eagerness to offer the best to these strangers who have appeared at his tent. But it is also somewhat ironic. How long does it take to slaughter a calf, prepare the meat, and then cook it? How long does it take to prepare the dough and make bread? This meal will not be fast food. Rather it will be the best that Abraham has available.

When the feast has been prepared, Abraham sets it before his guests and waits on them himself. Neither he nor Sarah share in the meal.

9"Where is your wife Sarah?" they asked him.
"There in the tent," he replied. 10One of them
said, "I will return to you about this time next year, and Sarah will then have a son."

Sarah, as a woman, has remained in the tent. She was inside as Abraham sat outside at the entrance. She no doubt heard the three visitors but did not see them. She was in the tent when Abraham asked her to make bread. Now the visitors ask Abraham where his wife is. This question is inappropriate, bordering on rude.

Visiting men do not ask about the host's wife. The men have been welcomed, refreshed, and fed. What is it they want with Abraham's wife? Abraham's response to them is curt, "There in the tent," only two words in the original Hebrew.

The men, however, are not to be put off. One of them—the reader by now realizes that this "one" is the Lord who was mentioned briefly in verse 1—makes a startling announcement. This apparent stranger declares that he will return in about a year and that Sarah will have given birth to a son. This time frame coincides with the same announcement in the previous chapter: "my covenant I will maintain with Isaac, whom Sarah shall bear to you by this time next year" (Gen 17:21).

The two announcements come from different writers and different time periods as was mentioned earlier. But in the text as it now stands the repetition reinforces the promise and adds some significant details. The announcement in Genesis 17 was made to Abraham. There is no indication that he revealed any of this message to Sarah. Now this announcement in Genesis 18 is made in Sarah's hearing. Sarah is listening, a fact that Abraham and the three visitors know.

Sarah was listening at the entrance of the tent, just behind him. 11Now Abraham and Sarah were old, advanced in years, and Sarah had stopped having her menstrual periods. 12So Sarah laughed to herself and said, "Now that I am worn out

and my husband is old, am I still to have sexual pleasure?"

The narrator in this chapter continues to focus on Sarah, mentioning that both Abraham and Sarah are old but adding other details. In chapter 17 Abraham laughs at the thought that a woman who is ninety years old could bear a child. But this narrator focuses on the woman's perspective: Sarah has ceased to have menstrual periods. Abraham laughed in Genesis 17; now Sarah laughs. What she says, however, is not that she is unable to bear a child. She notes that her husband is old and she cannot believe that she will still have sexual pleasure. The reader is left to ponder the implications of her statement.

When have God's plans caused you to laugh?

13But the LORD said to Abraham: "Why did Sarah laugh and say, 'Will I really bear a child, old as I am?' 14Is anything too marvelous for the LORD to do? At the appointed time, about this time next year, I will return to you, and Sarah will have a son."

Now the speaker is identified clearly. It is the Lord who responds. But the Lord speaks only to Abraham as is proper in this situation. Men in this culture do not talk to women who are hidden behind tent curtains. Nonetheless, the Lord has been listening to Sarah and asks, "Why did Sarah laugh?" In Genesis 17 God does not ask why Abraham laughed, but simply repeats the promise and insists that Sarah will be the mother of the anticipated son. But even though the Lord is paying attention to Sarah here, the repetition of Sarah's comment is revised. She did not say, "Will I really bear a child." She was more intent on what she observed of her husband's impotence because of age.

The Lord's reassurance to Abraham (and to Sarah behind the curtain) is consistent with the reassurance in chapter 17. Now the Lord asks a question: "Is anything too marvelous for the Lord to do?" Has Abraham, the man of faith, lost faith in the Lord's capability of giving him a son by Sarah? The awaited answer is no. Abraham and Sarah both may be too old for this to happen, but God has not lost the power of giving them a child. So the promise is repeated: "about this time next year, I will return to you, and Sarah will have a son." The word of God is powerful; when God speaks, the word is fulfilled. There are no more questions.

Where in your life is God telling you (directly or through others) that it's not too late for God to work marvels?

15 Sarah lied, saying, "I did not laugh," because she was afraid. But he said, "Yes, you did."

In Genesis 17 Abraham protested that God might not be able to accomplish this promise. Abraham knew he was in conversation with God. In Genesis 18 Sarah has no way of knowing that this stranger outside her tent is the Lord until she hears the question implying that the Lord can work any marvel. Now she knows that the announcement has been made by God. Now she is afraid because she laughed at the word of God. So she lies, denying that she laughed. God's response is direct: "Yes, you laughed."

The Bible delivers a consistent message about God's faithfulness and trustworthiness (Gen 21:1; Deut 7:9; Luke 1:45; 1 Cor 1:9; Heb 11:11). What do you think of Sarah's response? How do you respond when God acts in your life?

God does not seem offended by the laughter of either Abraham or Sarah. The promised son will arrive within the year: "The LORD took note of Sarah as he had said he would; the LORD did for her as he had promised" (Gen 21:1). Abraham names Sarah's son Isaac, which in Hebrew is a play on the word for "laughter." Sarah approves the name and announces with delight: "God has given me cause to laugh, and all who hear of it will laugh with me" (Gen 21:6). No story has a happier ending—at least at this point.

Praying the Word / Sacred Reading

Your promises, O God, reveal who you are and what you desire for us.
We come to know you as the Creator who breathes life into our universe,
the giver of the earth beneath our feet and the stars above our heads,
the author of our hearts' desires.
Like Sarah, may we be surprised by your presence in the daily routine of our lives,
and startled by the unexpected grace of long-held desires finding fulfillment.
Like Sarah and Abraham, may we be anchored by relationships where we discover
your message of hope and truth.
Give us the grace of offering hospitality so that we may see your face.

Grant us the attentiveness needed to hear your voice.
Fill us with laughter, a sign of deep and abiding joy,
evidence of hope in things not yet seen but believed.

Living the Word

Ultimately, Sarah was left to trust that God's will in her life would be fulfilled in a way that she could not control nor fully comprehend. Although she tried to control the way God's promised heirs would arrive, ultimately she waited on God to intervene in her life. Consider one desire or dream in your own life, one avenue where God seems to be leading you, but leading you more slowly than you wish. How might you make a concerted effort to wait on the signs of God's faithfulness? What will you do in this time of waiting? How might you prepare your heart as a place of hospitality for God to share with you?